A NewTune A Day ™
for Violin

The violin edition of *A New Tune A Day* is designed to be used seamlessly with the viola and cello editions. Teachers wishing to accommodate all instruments together in a lesson will be able to do so with almost every piece of every lesson, including the duets and rounds.

The few exceptions, in lesson 1, 2, and 7, are indicated as being specfic to the violin by the heading 'Violin Special':

look for this symbol within the book ✳

To access companion recorded performances and backing tracks, visit:
www.halleonard.com/mylibrary

Enter Code
7330-2796-6406-7734

THE BOSTON MUSIC COMPANY

DISTRIBUTED BY

HAL•LEONARD®

Foreword

Since its appearance in the early 1930s, C. Paul Herfurth's original *A Tune A Day* series has become the most popular instrumental teaching method of all time. Countless music students have been set on their path by the clear, familiar, proven material, and the logical, sensibly-paced progression through the lessons within the book.

The teacher will find that the new books have been meticulously rewritten by experienced teachers: instrumental techniques and practices have been updated and the musical content has been completely overhauled.

The student will find clearly-presented, uncluttered material, with familiar tunes and a gentle introduction to the theoretical aspects of music. The books are now accompanied by audio examples and backing tracks to help the student develop a sense of rhythm, intonation and performance at an early stage.

As in the original books, tests are given following every five lessons. Teachers are encouraged to present these as an opportunity to ensure that the student has a good overview of the information studied up to this point.

The following extract from the foreword to the original edition remains as true today as the day it was written:

The value of learning to count aloud from the very beginning cannot be over-estimated. Only in this way can a pupil sense rhythm.

Class teaching should be a combination of individual instruction and ensemble playing. At every lesson there should be individual playing so that all the necessary corrections can be made. Never allow pupils' mistakes to go unnoticed, since only by immediate correction will they develop the habit of careful thinking and playing.

Many teachers do the thinking for their pupils, instead of helping them to think for themselves. Insisting upon the mastery of each point will not dull their interest.

Music-making is a lifelong pleasure, and at its heart is a solid understanding of the principles of sound production and music theory. These books are designed to accompany the student on these crucial first steps: the rewards for study and practice are immediate and lasting. Welcome to the world of music!

Sincere thanks to Ginny Strawson for her invaluable help with this book.

Published by
Boston Music Company

Exclusive Distributors:
Hal Leonard
7777 West Bluemound Road, Milwaukee, WI 53213, USA.
Hal Leonard Europe Limited
42 Wigmore Street, Marylebone, London, W1U 2RN
Hal Leonard Australia Pty, Ltd.
4 Lentara Court, Cheltenham, Victoria, 3192 Australia.

This book © Copyright 2006 Boston Music Company,

Edited by David Harrison
Music processed by Paul Ewers Music Design
Original compositions and arrangements by Sarah Pope and Janet Coles
Cover and book designed by Chloë Alexander
Photography by Matthew Ward
Models: Martin Young
Printed in the United States of America
Backing tracks by Guy Dagul
Violin performances by Sarah Pope and Keith Lewis
Audio recorded, mixed and mastered by Jonas Persson and John Rose

Your Guarantee of Quality
As publishers, we strive to produce every book to the highest commercial
standards. The music has been freshly engraved and the book has been
carefully designed to minimize awkward page turns and to make playing
from it a real pleasure. Throughout, the printing and binding have been
planned to ensure a sturdy, attractive publication which should give years
of enjoyment. If your copy fails to meet our high standards, please inform
us and we will gladly replace it.

www.halleonard.com

Contents

Rudiments of music

The stave

Music is written on a grid of five lines called a *stave*.
At the beginning of each stave is placed a special symbol called a *clef* to describe the approximate range of the instrument for which the music is written.

This example shows a *treble clef*, generally used for melody instruments.

The stave is divided into equal sections of time, called *bars* or *measures*, by *barlines*.

Note values

Different symbols are used to show the time value of *notes*, and each *note value* has an equivalent symbol for a rest, representing silence.

The **quaver** (or *eighth note*), often used to signify a half beat, is written with a solid head and a stem with a tail. The quaver rest is also shown.

The **crotchet** (or *quarter note*), often used to signify one beat, is written with a solid head and a stem. The crotchet rest is also shown.

The **minim** (or *half note*) is worth two crotchets. It is written with a hollow head and a stem. The minim rest is placed on the middle line.

The **semibreve** (or *whole note*) is worth two minims. It is written with a hollow head. The semibreve rest hangs from the fourth line.

Other note values

Note values can be increased by half by adding a dot after the note head. Here a minim and a crotchet are together worth a *dotted* minim.

Grouping quavers

Where two or more quavers follow each other, they can be joined by a *beam* from stem to stem.

Time signatures

The number of beats in a bar is determined by the *time signature*, a pair of numbers placed after the clef.

The upper number shows how many beats each bar contains, whilst the lower number indicates what kind of note value is used to represent a single beat. This lower number is a fraction of a semibreve so that 4 represents crotchets and 8 represents quavers.

𝄫, for *common time*, is another way to write $\frac{4}{4}$.

$\frac{6}{8}$ means six quavers to the bar.

$\frac{4}{4}$ means four crotchets to the bar.

$\frac{3}{4}$ means three crotchets to the bar.

Note names

Notes are named after the first seven letters of the alphabet and are written on lines or spaces on the stave, according to pitch.

D E F G A B C D E F G

Accidentals

The pitch of a note can be altered up or down a half step (or *semitone*) by the use of sharp and flat symbols. These temporary pitch changes are known as accidentals.

The *sharp* (♯) raises the pitch of a note.

The *natural* (♮) returns the note to its original pitch.

The *flat* (♭) lowers the pitch of a note.

Ledger lines

Ledger lines are used to extend the range of the stave for low or high notes.

C B A G A B C D

Bar lines

Various different types of bar lines are used:

Double bar lines divide one section of music from another.

Final bar lines show the end of a piece of music.

Repeat marks show a section to be repeated.

Before you play:

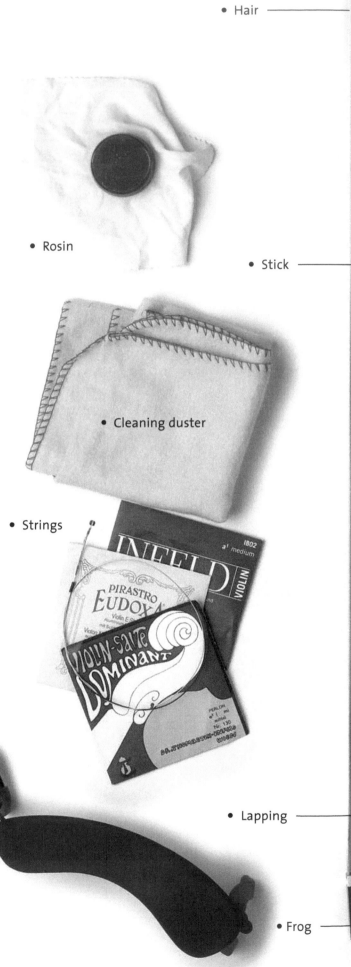

Accessories

Before your first violin lesson, make sure you have these items to go with your violin, bow and case:

- **Rosin** – derived from pine resin – to rub onto the bow hair before playing. It makes the hair sticky so that it grips the strings.

- **Duster** to remove rosin dust from the violin after playing.

- **Spare strings** come in packets identified by letter names and numbers:

  E = I   A = II   D = III   G = IV

  They are sold separately or in sets.

- **Chin rest** is usually attached to the violin when you buy it. Helps you hold the violin and protects it.
  Can be bought separately if you need a different design.

- **Shoulder rest** to help you hold the violin. There are many designs available. Ask your teacher.

- **Music stand**. Make sure you adjust it for your eye level – standing or sitting – so it will help you to develop good posture when playing.

- **Tuning assistance**. Violins frequently need to be tuned. See opposite for instructions: use a keyboard, an electronic tuner, or the tuning tracks on the accompanying audio to help you find the right note, or ask your teacher to show you how to use a tuning fork.

- Point
- Hair
- Rosin
- Stick
- Cleaning duster
- Strings
- Shoulder rest
- Lapping
- Frog
- Screw

- Scroll
- Pegs
- Neck
- Fingerboard
- Bridge
- F-hole
- Tailpiece
- Chin rest
- Fine-tuning adjuster

G A
D E

Tuning

Your teacher will show you how to tune your violin using the pegs and the fine-tuning adjusters. If your violin does not have adjusters it is a good idea to have them fitted because they are easier to use than the pegs. There may be a reason why your violin should not have them though, so check with your teacher or violin shop.

The pegs can be difficult to manage at first and need some practice. If you have the choice of pegs and adjusters, only use the pegs if the strings are very out of tune. Never tune the strings higher than the required note with the pegs or the strings are in danger of breaking. Tune to just below the note with the pegs then complete the fine tuning with the adjusters.

Most players tune the **A** string first as it is the common tuning note for orchestras and ensembles.

How to tune:

Sound a long A on your keyboard or accompanying online audio. Listen until you can sing or hum the A. You may have to try this a few times.

Now play the A string (pluck or bow), and sing the note it produces. Decide whether it sounds the same as the keyboard/audio note.

If the string sounds too low ('flat'), tighten the tuning adjuster by turning it clockwise. If the string sounds too high ('sharp'), loosen the tuning adjuster by turning it anticlockwise.

New strings can go out of tune quite quickly until they have been stretched to their required pitch for a while and "settle down".

Take care when carrying your violin because knocks and bumps can make it go out of tune.

Before you play:

Care of the violin and bow

Your violin is made of wood – usually maple and pine –
so beware:

COLD, DRY or DAMP can:
- Make it go out of tune
- Make it warp and crack

So keep your violin at an even temperature:

Never store your violin beside a heater
Never store your violin in a hot or cold parked car

If the instrument fits loosely in the case:
- Add some foam padding
- Make it a "blanket" and wrap it in a silk scarf.

Cleaning
Use a duster without polish, chemical products or water.

The bridge and soundpost are held in place by the tension
of the strings. They are not glued in position (to allow for
adjustment). Never take all the strings off at once or the
bridge and soundpost may become displaced.

The bow
After playing, remember to loosen the tension of the bow
to allow the stick to maintain its shape and flexibility.

Avoid touching the bow hair – or the bow will lose its grip.

Posture

Standing to play the violin allows easier balance and more freedom of movement than sitting.

Place the violin (with shoulder rest if you are using one) on your left collarbone.

Keep your natural body alignment – look straight ahead.

Drop the head slightly until the left side of the jaw meets the chin rest and you can hold the violin without raising your shoulder.

With fingers curved and thumb relaxed, rest the violin neck against the left thumb to share the weight of the violin with your left shoulder.

Avoid gripping the neck of the violin between finger and thumb.

Holding the bow

Make a circle with your 2nd finger overlapping the tip of the thumb.

Place the bow between 2nd finger and thumb and let the neighbouring fingers curve round the stick. The little fingertip rests on top of the stick.

goals:

1. **Name and play the open strings**
2. **Learn the value of minims and crotchets**

✳ **Part 1 – *Violin Special*: this section is not compatible with the cello book**

Pizzicato

Pizzicato is a technique used to play without the bow

Plucking the string, known as *pizzicato*, is a technique used to perform on the violin without the bow.

Use your right hand 1st finger and, resting your thumb against the fingerboard, pluck across the string with the fingertip (but don't use the nail).

Minims look like this: 𝅗𝅥 and are worth a count of **2**   **Crotchets** look like this: ♩ and are worth a count of **1**

Count: 1   2   3   4   1   2   3   4

Before you begin, count a steady '1, 2, 3, 4' several times and keep counting while you play.

Count: 1   2

 ## Exercise 1:

Play this exercise through several times until your pizzicato strokes are nice and even.

Count: 1   2   3   4

Sight-reading: Spell and play the following words

Pizzicato

A D D

Play the word   Spell and play

*Sight-reading
is an essential skill
for a musician.*

*You'll be surprised
how much easier this
becomes with practice.*

✳ **Part 2 – this section is compatible with the cello book**

Tambour on the D string

1. Try singing the tune on the lower line with your teacher.

2. Clap your line and count aloud.

3. Join in while your teacher plays the tune.

Student — *Pizzicato*

Count: 1   2   3   4   1   2   3   4

Teacher — *Arco*

*The same piece is
played here in two
different keys: once in
D and once in A.
Notice how, in the
first version, the
melody on the second
line of music seems to
come happily to rest
on the last note, D,
whereas in the second
example it's an A
that brings the piece
finally to a close.*

Tambour on the A string

Student — *Pizzicato*

Teacher — *Arco*

Pieces for Lesson 1

Tambour verse 2 on the D and A strings

1. Try singing the tune on the lower line with your teacher.

2. Clap your line and count aloud.

3. Join in while your teacher plays the tune.

Hoe Down

1. Try singing the tune on the lower line with your teacher.

2. Clap your line and count aloud.

3. Join in while your teacher plays the tune.

The rest symbol **━** in the empty bars indicates a whole bar's rest.

goals:

1. **Down bows and up bows**
2. **Using fast bow strokes**
3. **Bowing on crotchets and minims**

✳ **Part 1 – Violin Special: this section is not compatible with the cello book**

In the following pieces you will find bowing signs ⊓ and ∨ to help you plan your bow strokes. Make sure you have enough bow for long or short notes: use a longer bow stroke for long notes such as minims and a shorter stroke for short notes such as crotchets.

BOWING

⊓ *Down bow* means **pull** the bow to the **right**.

∨ *Up bow* means **push** the bow to the **left**.

Good posture will help you to retain a correct bowing technique.

Notice how bowing strokes alternate between ⊓ and ∨ .

Where no stroke is indicated, continue to alternate between up and down strokes.

Exercise 1:

In this piece, use quick alternating bow strokes. *Arco* means 'use the bow'.

Exercise 2:

Now use a mixture of short and long bow strokes to fit the rhythm of the words.

Pieces for Lesson 2

✱ **Part 2 – this section is compatible with the cello book**

Tambour verse 1

Frère Jacques

Now sing the tune of Frère Jacques.

Can you sing the tune and play the rhythm line on your violin at the same time?

Pieces for Lesson 2

Au Clair de la Lune

After the two bowing signs, continue with the alternating 'to & fro' actions for the rest of the piece.

Hoe Down

* (violin special)

Use short quick bow strokes

Long bows

3. **Name and play the notes E, F♯ and G on the D string, and the note B on the A string**

1. **Finger pattern one**
2. **Know the terms Pizzicato and Arco**

4. **Recognise the sharp sign** ♯

The fingers of the left hand are numbered, from 1 to 4, according to the picture below.

You will often find that violin music contains small numbers placed directly above the notes to indicate which finger should be used.

First finger on the D string

0 means play the string with **no** fingers on it (open), and **1** means use the first finger.

Sing the notes and then play *pizzicato*:

First finger on the A string

Hoe Down

Play this piece *pizzicato* at first, then try it *arco*:

keep 1st finger down

First, second and third fingers on the D string

Take a look at the pull-out fingering chart
to see where the sharps fall.

D E F♯ G G

*Notice how much
smaller the gap
between the 2nd
and 3rd fingers is
than between the
1st and 2nd.*

*You will learn more
about this in lesson 4.*

Keep each finger down as you go higher.

When you reach G with the 3rd finger, listen to make sure that it's in tune with the open G string.

Sight-reading

Spell and play the following words. The ♯ isn't part of the word!

Tambour (verse 1)

Play this piece *pizzicato* at first, then try it *arco*:

Merrily We Roll Along

Again, try this piece *pizzicato* at first, then play it *arco*:

Lesson 4

goals:

1. **New notes on the A string:** the D major scale
2. **Crotchet rests and minim rests**
3. **Re-takes**
4. **The semibreve**
5. **Time signatures**

Notice how the basic finger positions for the A string are the same as for the D string.

Notes on the A string

The finger pattern opposite shows a whole tone gap between the 1st and 2nd fingers, and a semitone between the 2nd and 3rd – which are close together. The distance of a tone is twice as wide as a semitone.

The major scale

The notes of the major scale follow a particular pattern of intervals.

Most of the notes are a tone apart, but between the 3rd and 4th notes of the scale, and again between the 7th and 8th notes of the scale, the interval is only half as much: a semitone.

Tone		Tone		Semitone		Tone		Tone		Tone		Semitone
1		2		3	4		5		6		7		8

D Major scale

Is the high D on the A string in tune with the open D string?

Crotchet and minim rests

Rests are silences.

Minim rests are shown like this:

Crotchet rests are shown like this:

Exercise 1: hand shape

Practise this piece for a consistent left hand shape.

Pieces for Lesson 4

Au Clair de la Lune

'Re-take' means: lift the bow and prepare for the next bow stroke in the same direction

re-take here

Notice the note symbol in the last bar: it is a semibreve, worth 4 crotchets.

Whose Cuckoo? (a round)

When you reach the end of this piece, play it again from the beginning.

re-take here   re-take here

A new player can begin every two bars.

Take a look at the information on time signatures in the Rudiments of Music section (pages 4 and 5).

The following pieces use time signatures giving either four beats or three beats in each bar.

London Bridge Is Falling Down

Play this piece pizzicato at first, then try it arco:

French Folk Song

This piece has three beats to the bar. The top number in the time signature indicates the number of beats.

Lesson 5

goals:

1. **Quavers**
2. **Key signatures**
3. **Repeats**

The pieces in this lesson feature quavers, each worth half a crotchet.

They are written singly with flags, and can be joined together with **beams**:

Learn to recognise patterns of notes and the rhythms they make: it will make sight-reading so much easier.

Pease Pudding Hot

Clap the rhythm and count aloud, then continue to count as you play.

The dots at the final barline are **repeat** markings: when you reach this sign go back to the beginning and play the piece for a second time.

Lavender's Blue

Key signatures

Often a piece of music contains some sharp signs at the beginning. This is the 'Key Signature'.

This sharp sign is on the F line of the stave. It means that all Fs in the music should be played as F♯.

This time there are sharp signs on the F line and in the C space: all the Fs will be F♯ and all the Cs will be C♯. This piece therefore uses the notes of the D major scale.

Pieces for Lesson 5

Frère Jacques (a round)

This piece has the key signature of D major.

A new player can begin every two bars.

Go From My Window

re-take here

A new player can begin every two bars.

Supplementary Pieces

Ave Maria (a round for 3 players)

A new player can begin every two bars..

Old Oxford (adapted)

Donkeys And Carrots (a round for 4 players)

re-take bow

re-take bow

Hee - Haw   Hee - Haw

A new player can begin every two bars..

Autumn (from the *Four Seasons*)

Vivaldi

1. Missing words

Write the missing words in this sentence:

We went to the .... and .... ordered some

.... It was ....

(4)

2. Rests

On the stave below, draw rests of the indicated duration:

| A whole bar | 2 beats | 1 beat | 3 beats |

(4)

3. Notes

On the stave below draw the following notes as minims:

G, B, E, C♯, A, D and **F♯**

(7)

4. Find the sharp notes

How many of these notes are sharps? _____ Check the key signature.

(5)

5. Fingers

Write the correct finger numbers above the notes:

(5)

Total (25)

Lesson 6

goals:

1. **Notes on the G string**
2. **Dynamics: loud and quiet**
3. **Repeats: first and second endings**
4. **Dotted minims**
5. **Whole bar's rest**
6. **Legato**

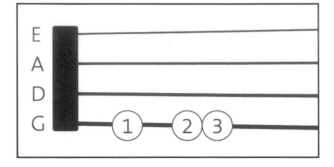

Notes on the G string

Notice how the fingers are placed in exactly the same way as for the D string and A string.

Dynamics

Music uses Italian words to describe how loudly or quietly to play.

These words or abbreviations are called 'Dynamic Markings'.

Forte (written as f) = **loud**

Piano (written as p) = **quiet**

Twinkle Twinkle Little Star

G major scale

Have a good look at the key signature and remember to play the correct sharps.

Try to sing the G major scale as you play it, and you'll find it has exactly the same 'melody' as the D major scale in lesson 4. It has the same sequence of tones and semitones.

24

Fingerboard   Neck   Peg   Scroll

Stick

Point

Finger Pattern 1

0

E STRING   E

A STRING   A

D STRING   D

G STRING   G

Tone

Finger Pattern 2

0

E STRING   E

A STRING   A

D STRING   D

G STRING   G

Tone

Finger Pattern 3

0   **1**
                                           (low)

E STRING   E   F

A STRING   A   B♭

D STRING   D   E♭

G STRING   G   A♭

Semitone

Chin rest   Tailpiece   Fine-tuning adjuster   Bridge   F-hole

G
D
A
E

Screw   Frog   Ferrule   Lapping   Hair

Pieces for Lesson 6

First and second endings

In the following piece play to the repeat mark including the 1st time ending and repeat from the beginning.

On the second time through the piece miss out the 1st time ending and play the 2nd time ending instead.

Start with an up bow at the point. On the repeat this will be a down bow.

The Can Can
Offenbach

Ode To Joy (from *Symphony no.9*)
Beethoven

legato means smoothly

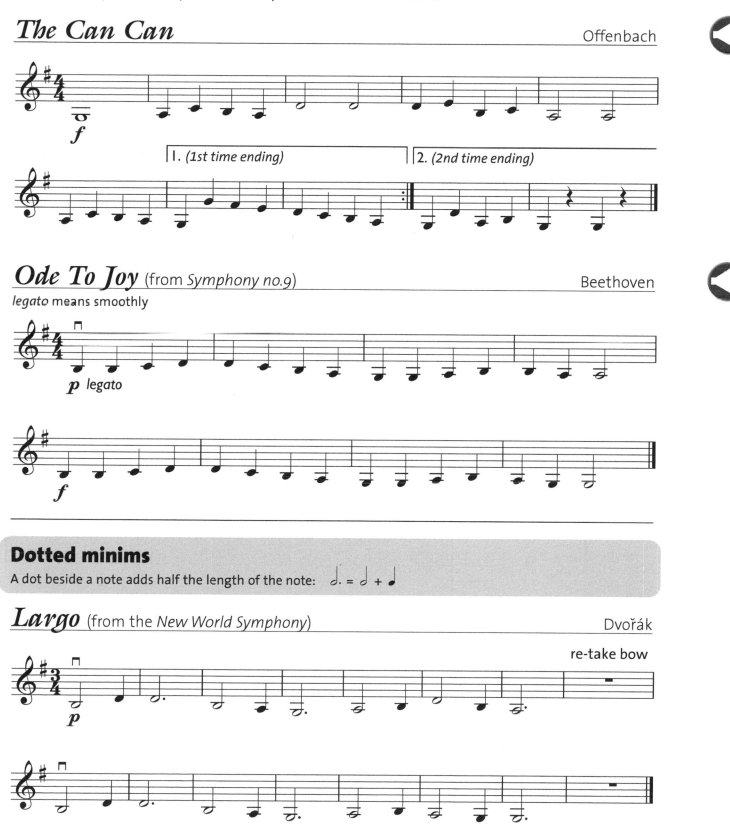

Dotted minims

A dot beside a note adds half the length of the note:

Largo (from the *New World Symphony*)
Dvořák

re-take bow

The rest symbol ▬ at the end of each line in this piece indicates a whole bar's rest.

goals:

1. **Notes on the E string**
2. **Up beats**
3. **Tied notes**

* **Violin Special: this lesson is *not* compatible with the cello book**

Here's the same pattern again — and this time a tone following the F♯ means that the G is also sharpened.

Notes on the E string

Here is the familiar finger pattern, this time for the E string.

Tied notes

A note can be extended by tying it to another note of the same pitch.

This is shown by a curved line, joining two notes that make one continuous sound.

Notice how, in the following example, the bottom line uses notes longer than the length of a whole bar.

These long tied open string notes, played along with the melody, sound rather like droning bagpipes.

Skye Boat Song

Scottish traditional

A major scale

Pieces for Lesson 7

Country Garden

Up beats

Sometimes a piece of music doesn't begin with a whole bar. The remaining pieces on this page all begin with a single beat representing the last beat of a bar. This short bar at the beginning (called an **up beat** or **anacrusis**) should be balanced by another short bar at the end. The two short bars together add up to a whole bar.

The Happy Farmer

Schumann

Amazing Grace

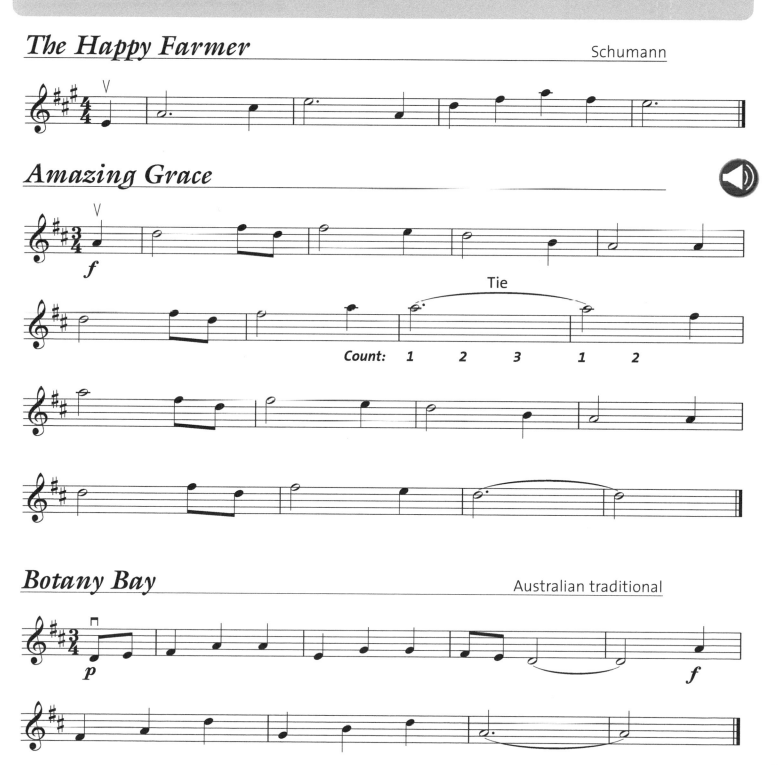

Tie

Count: 1   2   3   1   2

Botany Bay

Australian traditional

Lesson 8 goals:

1. **Finger pattern 2**
2. **C major scale**
3. **G major scale: 2nd octave**
4. **New dynamics:** *mp* and *mf*

The C major scale requires no sharps in the key signature.

Notice how the Fs and Cs are natural: they are played a semitone lower than the F♯ and C♯ that you have played up until now.

Compare the positions of Cs and Fs in the diagram opposite with the previous patterns.

C major scale

New dynamics

mp = mezzo piano, meaning moderately quiet
    (mezzo literally means 'half')

mf = mezzo forte, meaning moderately loud

Botany Bay

Do you remember this tune in lesson 7? It was higher, using the notes of the D major scale.

Now here is the whole tune, one note lower, using the notes of the C major scale.

G major scale: second octave

You will have noticed that certain notes are given the same name despite having different pitches.

The scale below begins with the G that is an octave (8 notes) higher than the open 4th string, and continues up to the G on the E string: another octave higher.

The new finger pattern is used here on the E string, too.

High and low second fingers

Don't forget to check your finger pattern.

Is your 2nd finger close to the 3rd finger or close to the 1st finger?

When the 2nd finger is close to the 3rd finger it is 'high', and when it's close to the 1st finger it's 'low'.

Pieces for Lesson 8

Andante (from the Surprise Symphony)

Haydn

Grandfather's Clock

Common time

The $\frac{4}{4}$ time signature is often referred to as common time, and can be written like this: **C**

Jingle Bells

New dynamics

ff = fortissimo, meaning very loud

Hark! The Herald Angels Sing

This piece is marked mf at the beginning. Don't start too loudly or you won't be able to build to a proper fortissimo by the end.

Slurs

Slurring – playing two or more notes with the same bow direction – is an important bowing technique.

Slur symbols look just like ties, but they join two or more notes of different pitches.

legato

Slurs across strings

1 keep 1st finger down

2 keep 2nd finger down   **3** keep 3rd finger down

Unto Us A Child Is Born

We Three Kings

Now practise slurring three notes to a single bow.

legato

Music can gradually become louder or quieter, and the following Italian words are used to show this:

Crescendo – gradually louder   *Diminuendo* – gradually quieter

Good King Wenceslas

f

p   crescendo   *ff*

Start growing louder from the *p* marking until the *ff*.

Lesson 10 goals:

1. Dotted crotchet
2. Dynamics: pianissimo
3. Crescendo and diminuendo 'hairpin' symbols
4. Repeated sections

Dotted crotchet rhythm

A dot beside a crotchet adds half the length of the note: ♩. = ♩ + ♪

Exercise 1:

First, clap and count each of the following three lines, then play and count them.

Lines (b) and (c) should sound the same.

Notice how the same rhythm can be written in different ways. Get used to seeing patterns rather than reading each individual note.

Your performance will flow better and your sight-reading will improve.

Silent Night

Gruber

Remember: the 2nd beat starts on the 'dot' of the first crotchet.

Count: 1 + 2 + 3 +

Hairpins

Crescendo and diminuendo passages are often indicated by long 'hairpins' placed horizontally beneath the music.

While Shepherds Watched Their Flocks

This hairpin means *crescendo*

This hairpin means *diminuendo*

Pieces for Lesson 10

Deck The Halls

Count: 1 + 2 + 3 + 4 +

The First Noël

mf

f (second time)

re-take bow

Notice that, since the repeated section doesn't start at the beginning of the piece, a separate repeat mark is needed for each end of the repeated section.

New dynamics   *pp* = *pianissimo* meaning very quiet

Silent Night

pp

p

mp

We Wish You A Merry Christmas

f   *ff*

Supplementary Pieces

We Three Kings

Once In Royal David's City

Deck The Halls

Skaters' Waltz

Waldteufel

1. Note duration

On the stave below, draw notes of the indicated duration:

one quaver   two beats-worth of quavers   dotted crotchet   a note that lasts three beats

(8)

2. Scale

On the stave below, draw the A major scale including the correct key signature:

(4)

3. Notes

On the stave below draw the following notes as crotchets:

F, A, B, C♯, F♯, D, G and **E**

(4)

4. Dynamics

What are the Italian words for:

Moderately loud _____

Moderately quiet _____

(4)

5. Naming ceremony

What do these Italian words mean?   What do these signs mean?

legato   ***pp***

arco   ***mf***

crescendo   **c**

pizzicato

diminuendo   :‖

(5)

Total (25)

goals:

1. **Spiccato-lifted bow strokes**
2. **Tempo markings**

Spiccato

Try to visualise the bow movement as a little smile, beginning with the approach to the string and ending as the bow lifts off again.

This needs to be controlled and consistent.

Spiccato is a short, lifted bow stroke used to produce a detached (*staccato*) note.

Find a place in the lower half of the bow that gives you maximum control, and draw a smile with your bow as you lift it off the string.

Spiccato notes are marked like this:

Oats And Beans

Find the best part of the bow to control the landing and lifting.

Did you find the best part of the bow?

Italian terms are often used to indicate the speed (tempo) of a piece:

Andante – at walking pace   *Moderato* – moderately

Allegretto – fairly quickly   *Allegro* – quickly

Andante (from the Surprise Symphony)

Haydn

Did you remember to lift the bow off the string?

Pieces for Lesson 11

Moderato (from the Peasant's Cantata)

Bach

lift bow to finish

Did you remember to lift the bow off the string?

When you make spiccato bow strokes cushion your landings with flexible fingers and wrist.

London's Burning (a round)

A new player can begin every two bars.

Reuben And Rachel (a round for two players)

Allegretto

re-take for repeat

A new player can begin after one bar.

Yankee Doodle

Allegro

Lesson 12

goals:

1. Hooked bowings (broken slurs)
2. Quaver rests
3. Pause sign
4. Ritenuto

Hooked bowing

Hooked bowing means playing two or more detached notes in the same bow direction.

It is usually written with a slur between two notes and lines on the noteheads, as in the example below.

Exercise 1:

Stop the bow after each note

This sign ⌢ is called a **pause** (or *fermata*). When this sign appears, the note should be held for longer than usual. The pause sign is sometimes found at the end of a piece of music.

Scarborough Fair

Skye Boat Song

Allegretto

re-take bow

re-take bow

(2nd time)

Pieces for Lesson 12

Allegro (from Spring from the *Four Seasons*)

Vivaldi

Remember the 'hooked' bowing

1st time *f*
2nd time *p*

re-take

f

p

mf

f

Quaver rests

Quaver rests are shown like this:

> **Rit.** – *ritenuto*. Literally meaning 'held back', *rit.* is used to slow the tempo of a piece temporarily, adding to the dramatic effect.

Nessun Dorma

Puccini

Find the best part of the bow to start. Will you have enough bow for the semibreve?

lift bow for re-take

Count: 1 + 2 + 3 + 4 +

rit.

When The Saints Go Marching In

Allegro

lift bow   lift bow

Count: 1 + 2 + 3 + 4 +

lift bow

goals:

1. **Arpeggios**
2. **Composing a round**

Arpeggios

Have a look at the pieces of music in this book, and you'll discover that melodies are generally made from a combination of fragments of arpeggios and scale passages.

Practise both scales and arpeggios regularly, and you'll find it much easier to tackle new pieces of music.

Arpeggios are made by playing the first, third and fifth notes of a scale in sequence.

Many melodies have sections containing arpeggios. Scales and arpeggios should be practised regularly.

D major scale

Notice how Roman numerals are used to show the degree of the scale, and that the eighth note – the octave – is numbered the same as the first note.

D major arpeggio

The major arpeggio sounds like the first four notes of 'Morning Has Broken', reproduced opposite in G as the original Gaelic melody 'Bunessan'.

Sing this arpeggio first, then play it:

Now use the same finger pattern to play arpeggios starting on the G or A strings.

Fanfare (a round)

A new player can begin every half bar.

Now try making your own round using notes from an arpeggio of your choice.

Choose a rhythm pattern with 2, 3, or 4 beats to the bar, and write in the time signature.

Pieces for Lesson 13

Kumbayah

Notice how, in the second line, a new time signature is introduced for a single bar.

Ecossaise

Beethoven

Bunessan (Gaelic melody)

Lesson 14 goals:

1. **F major scale and arpeggio**
2. **Low 1st finger on the A and E strings.**
3. **Low 2nd finger on the G string.**

You have learnt to play sharps in previous lessons and now you'll be looking at flats. How many different keys have you studied in this book? How would you go about playing some of the pieces in a different key?

The flat sign (♭) to the left of a note-head lowers the note by a semitone.

In the following scale the B is played as a B♭ to play the major scale: **T - T - S - T - T - T - S**

F major scale

F major arpeggio

In the key of F, a low 2nd finger is needed on the G string.

Keep the hand in its shape over the string as you play the low first finger.

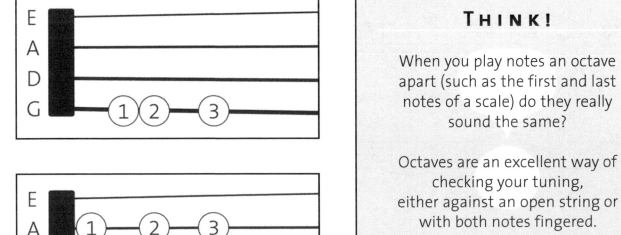

THINK!

When you play notes an octave apart (such as the first and last notes of a scale) do they really sound the same?

Octaves are an excellent way of checking your tuning, either against an open string or with both notes fingered.

Pieces for Lesson 14

Filou

Praetorius

Allegro

mf

Abide With Me

Monk

Andante

mp

crescendo

mf

The Happy Farmer

Schumann

Allegro

f

Lullaby

Brahms

In this piece a low 2nd finger on the G string will be required for the B♭.

Andante

pp

low 2nd finger

further techniques:

Tremolo

This is a technique using very quick bowing to create a shimmering sound.

It is indicated in music with lines over note stems like this: 𝄐

Play *tremolo* with very fast little bow strokes near the point of the bow.

Gymnopédie No. 1

Satie

Mysteriously

tremolo here

Skye Boat Song

In this piece, play both the D and A strings all the time.

Playing notes on two strings together is known as *double stopping*.

Harmonics

Try sliding your left hand all the way up the D string and then back down, touching the string very lightly with your 4th finger as you go. Bow near the bridge as you slide the finger and you will hear some strange ethereal sounds. These are the notes of the harmonic series.

If you place your 4th finger very lightly on the D string halfway to the bridge and play with a fast bowstroke near the bridge you will hear a flute-like ringing note one octave above the open D string: the octave harmonic.

Try sliding up to the octave harmonic as shown below.

Harmonics are indicated by a little circle over the note-head. Try this technique on all your strings.

Pieces for Lesson 15

Lovely Evening (a round for three players)

Moderato

A new player can begin every six bars.

Sumer Is Icumen In (a round)

Allegro

Slide the hand now

A new player can begin every four bars.

re-take

Seagulls

Slide your left hand all the way to the top
of any string.

Now press the string down with your 4th finger
and slide it down the string fast, lots of times,
for about a centimetre.

Use a fast down bow for each slide, re-taking after
each stroke. You will sound like a flock of seagulls!

Supplementary Pieces

for Lessons 11 to 15

1. Key signatures

On the stave below, draw the correct key signatures for:

G major   F major   A major   D major   C major

(5)

2. Dots

Simplify the music on the left using dots to get rid of the ties

(5)

3. Arpeggios

a: Put a ring round the notes that make an arpeggio

b: Which scale is this?

(6)

4. Terms

What do the following terms mean:

Allegretto _____   Fermata _____

Spiccato _____   Ritenuto _____

(4)

5. Naming ceremony

Identify all the items indicated by arrows.

(5)

Total (25)

Online Audio Guide

1 Tuning Note G
2 Tuning Note D
3 Tuning Note A
4 Tuning Note E
5 Virtuoso Performance
6 Lesson 1 Exercise 1 *Demonstration*
7 Lesson 1 Exercise 1 *Backing Only*
8 Tambour on the D string *Demonstration*
9 Tambour on the D string *Backing Only*
10 Hoe Down *Demonstration*
11 Hoe Down *Backing Only*
12 Lesson 2 Exercise 1 *Demonstration*
13 Lesson 2 Exercise 1 *Backing Only*
14 Frère Jacques *Demonstration*
15 Frère Jacques *Backing Only*
16 Au Clair de la Lune *Demonstration*
17 Au Clair de la Lune *Backing Only*
18 Hoe Down *Demonstration*
19 Hoe Down *Backing Only*
20 Merrily We Roll Along *Demonstration*
21 Merrily We Roll Along *Backing Only*
22 London Bridge Is Falling Down *Demonstration*
23 London Bridge Is Falling Down *Backing Only*
24 French Folk Song *Demonstration*
25 French Folk Song *Backing Only*
26 Lavender's Blue *Demonstration*
27 Lavender's Blue *Backing Only*
28 Go From My Window *Demonstration*
29 Go From My Window *Backing Only*
30 Old Oxford *Demonstration*
31 Old Oxford *Backing Only*
32 Autumn *Demonstration*
33 Autumn *Backing Only*
34 The Can Can *Demonstration*

35 The Can Can *Backing Only*
36 Ode To Joy *Demonstration*
37 Ode To Joy *Backing Only*
38 Country Garden *Demonstration*
39 Country Garden *Backing Only*
40 Amazing Grace *Demonstration*
41 Amazing Grace *Backing Only*
42 Botany Bay *Demonstration*
43 Botany Bay *Backing Only*
44 Andante *Demonstration*
45 Andante *Backing Only*
46 Jingle Bells *Demonstration*
47 Jingle Bells *Backing Only*
48 Unto Us A Child Is Born *Demonstration*
49 Unto Us A Child Is Born *Backing Only*
50 Good King Wenceslas *Demonstration*
51 Good King Wenceslas *Backing Only*
52 While Shepherds Watched Their Flocks *Demonstration*
53 While Shepherds Watched Their Flocks *Backing Only*
54 The First Noël *Demonstration*
55 The First Noël *Backing Only*
56 Silent Night *Demonstration*
57 Silent Night *Backing Only*
58 We Three Kings *Demonstration*
59 We Three Kings *Backing Only*
60 Once In Royal David's City *Demonstration*
61 Once In Royal David's City *Backing Only*
62 Deck The Halls *Demonstration*
63 Deck The Halls *Backing Only*
64 Skaters' Waltz *Demonstration*
65 Skaters' Waltz *Backing Only*
66 Moderato *Demonstration*
67 Moderato *Backing Only*
68 Yankee Doodle *Demonstration*
69 Yankee Doodle *Backing Only*
70 Scarborough Fair *Demonstration*
71 Scarborough Fair *Backing Only*

72 Skye Boat Song *Demonstration*
73 Skye Boat Song *Backing Only*
74 Allegro *Demonstration*
75 Allegro *Backing Only*
76 Nessun Dorma *Demonstration*
77 Nessun Dorma *Backing Only*
78 When The Saints Go Marching In *Demonstration*
79 When The Saints Go Marching In *Backing Only*
80 Ecossaise *Demonstration*
81 Ecossaise *Backing Only*
82 Bunessan *Demonstration*
83 Bunessan *Backing Only*
84 Abide With Me *Demonstration*
85 Abide With Me *Backing Only*
86 Lullaby *Demonstration*
87 Lullaby *Backing Only*
88 Gymnopédie No1 *Demonstration*
89 Gymnopédie No1 *Backing Only*
90 Skye Boat Song *Demonstration*
91 Sumer Is Icumen In *Demonstration*
92 Theme from First Symphony (Brahms) *Demonstration*
93 Theme from First Symphony (Brahms) *Backing Only*
94 Auld Lang Syne *Demonstration*
95 Auld Lang Syne *Backing Only*

How to use the online audio

The tuning notes 1-4 are the notes of the open strings on the violin, beginning with the lowest string. The virtuoso performance gives an idea of how the violin can sound. The backing tracks are listed in the order in which they appear in the book. Look for the symbol in the book for the relevant backing track.